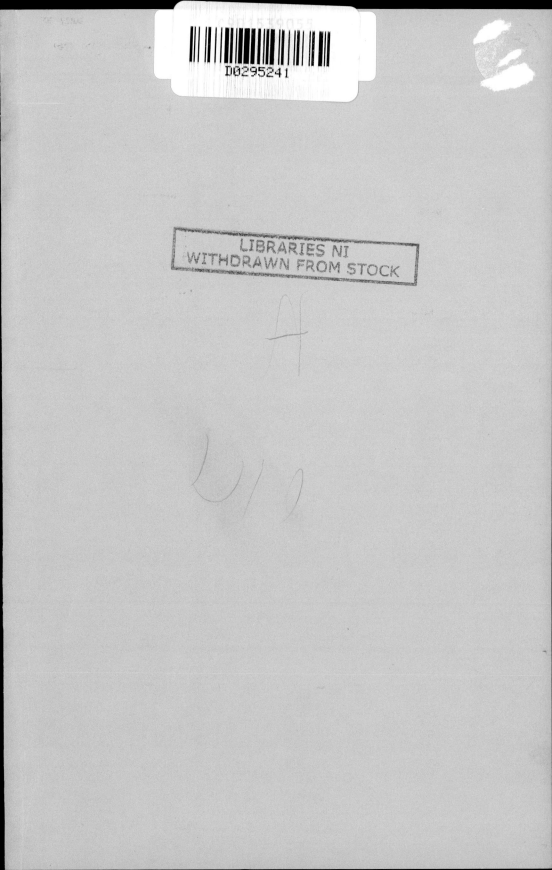

Welcome to the
Disney Learning Programme!

Sharing a book with your child is the perfect opportunity to cuddle and enjoy the reading experience together. Research has shown that reading aloud with your child is one of the most important ways to prepare them for success as a reader. When you share books with each other, you help strengthen your child's reading and vocabulary skills as well as stimulate their curiosity, imagination and enthusiasm for reading.

In this book meet Princess Anna, and learn all about what makes her different from her sister Elsa. Are they so different they can't be friends? You can enhance the reading experience by talking to your child about their own experiences with a sibling or friend. How are they different to them? Can those differences be a good thing? Children find it easier to understand what they read when they can connect it with their own personal experiences.

Children learn in different ways and at different speeds, but they all require a supportive environment to nurture a lifelong love of books, reading and learning. The *Adventures in Reading* books are carefully levelled to present new challenges to developing readers. They are filled with familiar and fun characters from the wonderful world of Disney to make the learning experience comfortable, positive and enjoyable.

Enjoy your reading adventure together!

Scholastic Children's Books
Euston House,
24 Eversholt Street,
London NW1 1DB, UK

A division of Scholastic Ltd
London • New York • Toronto • Sydney • Auckland
Mexico City • New Delhi • Hong Kong

This book was first published in Australia in 2015 by Scholastic Australia.
This edition published in the UK by Scholastic Ltd in 2015.

ISBN 978 1 4071 6300 0

Printed in Malaysia

2 4 6 8 10 9 7 5 3 1

Papers used by Scholastic Children's Books are made from woods grown in sustainable forests.

www.scholastic.co.uk

From the movie
DISNEY
FROZEN

DISNEY
LEARNING

LEVEL 1

Meet Anna

ADVENTURES IN READING

Based on the story *A Sister More Like Me*
by Barbara Jean Hicks
Illustrated by Brittney Lee

Anna is a princess. She has
red hair and rosy cheeks.
She likes bright colours
and lots of noise.

Anna has a sister.
Her name is Elsa.
Elsa is Anna's big sister.

The sisters live in a royal castle
in Arendelle. The castle is
enormous, and very, very old.

Anna has always lived in the kingdom of Arendelle. When she was a little girl, she played outside with her sister.

Elsa had magic powers.
She could make ice and snow!
She made a snowman called Olaf.

Anna and Olaf had lots of fun together. Olaf was made of cold snow, but Anna could give him a warm hug.

Anna always wanted to play with Elsa. But one day, Elsa stopped wanting to play with Anna.

Elsa was scared of playing with Anna.
She was worried that her magic
powers would hurt Anna.
So Elsa hid herself away.

The sisters spent a lot of time apart.
They didn't speak to each other.
They became very different.

Anna liked to joke and play games.
She still wanted to play with Elsa.
But Elsa was always too scared.

Anna learned to have fun on her own. She rode her pony every day. Even the rain would not stop Anna from playing outside!

Now Anna has grown up, but
she still loves to be outside.
She loves to climb up high
and feel the wind in her hair.

Elsa has grown up too. She is not scared of her magic any more. Elsa no longer stays away from her little sister.

Anna and Elsa do things differently.
But they can still have fun together!

Anna is so happy to have a sister like Elsa.